EXTREME SPORTS

BMX RACING

BY THOMAS K. ADAMSON

EPIC

BELLWETHER MEDIA • MINNEAPOLIS, MN

EPIC BOOKS are no ordinary books. They burst with intense action, high-speed heroics, and shadows of the unknown. Are you ready for an Epic adventure?

This edition first published in 2016 by Bellwether Media, Inc.

No part of this publication may be reproduced in whole or in part without written permission of the publisher. For information regarding permission, write to Bellwether Media, Inc., Attention: Permissions Department, 5357 Penn Avenue South, Minneapolis, MN 55419.

Library of Congress Cataloging-in-Publication Data

Adamson, Thomas K., 1970-
  BMX Racing / by Thomas K. Adamson.
    pages cm. – (Epic: Extreme Sports)
  Summary: "Engaging images accompany information about BMX racing. The combination of high-interest subject matter and light text is intended for students in grades 2 through 7"–Provided by publisher.
  Audience: Ages 7 to 12
  Includes bibliographical references and index.
  ISBN 978-1-62617-274-6 (hardcover: alk. paper)
  1. Bicycle motocross–Juvenile literature. I. Title.
  GV1049.3.A33 2016
  796.622–dc23
                    2015007777

Printed in the United States of America, North Mankato, MN.

TABLE OF CONTENTS

WARNING
The riders in this book are professionals. Always wear a helmet and other safety gear when you are on a bike.

OLYMPIC GOLD

Maris Strombergs and seven other BMX racers wait at the top of the starting hill. They all stand on their pedals. The gate drops. The racers take off!

London 2012

GOOD BALANCE
Riders balance on both pedals to get a faster start.

Finish

QUICK RACING

BMX races in the Olympics are over quickly. The winner usually finishes in under 40 seconds.

6

The racers speed over the jumps. Strombergs edges ahead of the other riders to take the lead. He stays at the front for the rest of the race. He wins his second straight Olympic BMX gold medal!

BMX RACING

BMX stands for bicycle motocross. BMX racers speed around tight turns on small bikes. Their goal is to cross the finish line first.

The tracks are often made of dirt and **asphalt**. They include **obstacles** to **challenge** the racers. Racers go over rollers, table tops, and a rhythm section. Berms allow them to pedal fast around turns.

table top

rhythm section

BMX RACING TERMS

berms—banked turns that allow racers to keep their speed

gate—the short wall at the start line that drops at the beginning of a race

motos—BMX races

rhythm section—a series of small jumps

rollers—small hills

starting hill—the steep hill that gives racers a burst of speed to start the race

table tops—jumps with flat tops

BMX BEGINNINGS

Motocross racing became popular in the 1960s and 1970s. Kids wanted to **imitate** motorcycle racing stars. They raced their bikes on dirt tracks.

OLD NAME

BMX racing was first called pedal-cross.

DOWNHILL BMX

The X Games used to have a BMX racing event. Riders competed in Downhill BMX from 2001 to 2003.

Kids began making their bikes faster. Soon, races were **organized** into **competitions**. They had created a new sport!

BMX GEAR

All BMX racers wear helmets. BMX **jerseys** and pants have pads to protect riders during falls. Gloves keep their hands safe from **road rash**.

THE COMPETITION

BMX events are organized into series of races called motos. Each moto has up to eight riders. BMX racers compete against others of the same age and **ability**.

EVENT SCORING

BMX racers earn points for top finishes. These points are added up over the season. The racer with the most points wins the track championship.

There are four motos to begin the event. The top four finishers of each moto move on to the next round. Then the top three racers in the final moto win medals!

INNOVATOR OF THE SPORT

name: Brandon Meadows
birthdate: March 24, 1981
hometown: Sacramento, California
innovations: Won the X Games gold medal in Downhill BMX in 2001 and 2003

GLOSSARY

ability—skill level

asphalt—a hard black substance used in the turns on BMX tracks; asphalt is also used to make roads.

challenge—to test

competitions—events where people race to win

imitate—to copy

jerseys—shirts with padding to protect riders

obstacles—bumps and jumps that challenge BMX riders

organized—planned ahead of time

road rash—scrapes on the skin from sliding on a rough surface

TO LEARN MORE

AT THE LIBRARY

Anderson, A.J. *BMX Biking*. Mankato, Minn.: Smart Apple Media, 2013.

Cohn, Jessica. *BMX*. New York, N.Y.: Gareth Stevens Pub., 2013.

Stuckey, Rachel. *Ride It BMX*. New York, N.Y.: Crabtree Pub., 2012.

ON THE WEB

Learning more about BMX racing
is as easy as 1, 2, 3.

1. Go to www.factsurfer.com.

2. Enter "BMX racing" into the search box.

3. Click the "Surf" button and you will see a list
   of related web sites.

With factsurfer.com, finding more information
is just a click away.

INDEX

The images in this book are reproduced through the courtesy of: homydesign, front cover, pp. 9, 11, 15; Matt Rourke/ AP/ Corbis, p. 4; Li Ga/ Xinhua Press/ Corbis, p. 5; Christophe Ena/ AP/ Corbis, pp. 6, 16, 18-19; Tim de Waele/ Corbis, pp. 7, 10; Jeff Siner/ MCT/ Newscom, pp. 8-9; Mirrorpix/ Newscom, pp. 12-13; Associated Press, p. 14; MarcelClemens, p. 17; Clifford White/ Corbis, p. 19; Thomas van Bracht/ Demotix/ Corbis, p. 20; Tony Donaldson/ Icon SMI/ Newscom, p. 21 (top, bottom).